Family Healing Journal

Sydney,
You're awesome! So happy
to know you.
go forth & prosper!
Ve——

PRAISES

For the book, *Becoming the Mom I Wish I'd Had...*

This book is full of practical wisdom for anyone wishing to be the best parent that you can be. If you want emotionally healthy, creative, confident, loving, responsible children, buy this book and heed Venus Taylor's sage advice. I am recommending it to every parent I know.

Susan Campbell, Ph.D.
Author of Getting Real, Saying What's Real, and
The Couples Journey
www.susancampbell.com

I can't put the book...down.
[It] is a MUST read for every mom and future mom. Even those who have not come from abusive homes, repeat patterns that their parents did, etc.
It really makes you mindful of how we parent, and conscious of how important our job of mom really is

S. Resnicoff
Lakewood, NJ

[This] book has touched my heart so deeply.
I've been lamenting the gulf between my desire to have close relationships with my children, and the reality of the distance that some of my shortcomings create.
Your book is such a compassionate, wise and practical response to this chasm. I am continuing to work through the exercises...
I think that it will be well-appreciated by parents in all stages of the child-rearing journey.

J. James-Carnes
New London, CT

For Venus Taylor, Founder of The Family Healing Institute…

Venus has allowed me to see things within myself in a gentle nonthreatening way. Interacting with her has allowed me to have more patience with my children and to allow them to be who they are.

N. Muhammad
Boston, MA

Her compassion, devotion to family and generous nature will help support…families in a crisis… [or just] in need of a friend and counselor.

L. Mitchell
Roxbury, MA

Venus has the ability to listen beneath the words and hear what is being felt as well as expressed. She has the courage to share what she has gleaned and gently push one to action.

A. James-Curtis
Flossmoor, IL

[Venus] is very insightful and knowledgeable in all areas applicable to coaching, relationships, success, abundance and personal empowerment.

We all create our 'stories' which can keep us stuck in repeating patterns.

Venus can help you get to the bottom of your 'story' so you can become who it is you are really wanting to be, and thus achieve your highest goals.

R. Reid
Arlington, MA

Family Healing Journal

A Companion to
Becoming the Mom I Wish I'd Had: How to Heal Yourself and Your Family Through HEART-Based Parenting

Venus Taylor, Ed.M.

Lower Mills Publishing Company
Dorchester, Massachusetts

Author portrait by Carol Lundeen
Cover design by Vaughan Davidson

Published by Lower Mills Publishing Company
www.lowermillspublishing.com

www.HealMyFamily.com
venus@HealMyFamily.com

First Edition, June 2009
ISBN 978-0-9823186-4-5 (Paperback)

10 9 8 7 6 5 4 3 2 1

~ TABLE OF CONTENTS ~

~ A NOTE TO FELLOW TRAVELERS ~

This is YOUR SPACE. In these pages, you are invited to explore your memories of childhood and your dreams of parenthood.

Be honest, in this space, about what you feel and what you want.

If there is healing to do, then face the pain boldly in these pages. Much like the "monster in the closet," when you muster up the courage to face pain and fear, to fully experience it without denial or avoidance, you may find it's much less scary than you imagined.

Feelings that are suppressed remain with us. They are expressed in unhealthy ways. They control us unconsciously.

Feelings that are explored eventually pass. Once they are acknowledged and respected, we no longer build identities around them. We can let our feelings come and go, while making conscious, healthy choices about how to move forward.

Conscious, emotionally healthy parents are better able to raise conscious, emotionally healthy children.

Your commitment to parenting from the HEART (with Honesty, Empathy, Appreciation, Respect, and Time), instead of from a place of POWER (Promoting Obedience While Encouraging Resentment), is the greatest contribution you can make to World Peace: Happy, Confident, Self-Managing Young People.

Use this journal to design your conscious approach to parenting. Let it be your reference as you Parent With the End in Mind.

I've left blank spaces, instead of lines, so you can feel free to create in the way that best suits you: large print, small print, pictures, diagrams.

If you feel like you could use some support on your journey of self- and family-healing, find me at www.HealMyFamily.com. I am passionate about helping parents (and couples) create homes where everyone feels seen, heard, understood, and respected.

Enjoy the Journey!
Venus

~ Part I ~

Looking Back:

Putting The Past

To Work For You

Chapter 1

Exploring Your Mom's Mistakes

Those who cannot learn from history are doomed to repeat it
~ George Santayana ~.

To avoid repeating history – to avoid handing down any legacy of pain we have inherited – it behooves us to study it.

There is a bounty of mothering wisdom in any emotional baggage we may have lugged from childhood into adulthood.

Use the Trial-to-Treasure process to sift through any painful childhood memories – large or small – and find the golden-nugget insights to help you become a more conscious, sensitive, supportive parent.

The 3 steps are as follows:

1. Revisit the Memory
2. Acknowledge the Effects
3. Uncover the Treasure

Let's cover the painful memories in this chapter. We'll enjoy the happier memories in Chapter 2.

Trial-to-Treasure Step 1: Revisit the Memory

Let's unpack the baggage one story at a time. You may want to go to a quiet, private space. Take a journal or a voice recorder – or a close friend if you like – and **jot down your answers and observations**.

If it's too painful to go back in first person, try seeing each scene as if it's happening to someone else. Watch the movie of what happened as if through a camera lens. You can zoom in or zoom way out based on how safe you feel reviewing the film.

❖ ❖ ❖ ❖ ❖ ❖ ❖ ❖ ❖ ❖ ❖ ❖ ❖ ❖ ❖

Exercise 1.1: Revisit the Painful Memory

Examine the painful memory you replay in your mind most often.

The event may have been major – life-threatening, sanity-threatening – or a relatively small injustice. When you were a kid, so small and vulnerable, it may have felt very painful on some level. Respect your childhood perspective. Don't belittle it.

Do your best to actually see, in your mind's eye, what happened. Take a good, loving look at the little girl that was you.

What's happening to her in this scene?

How is she (the little-girl you) feeling? *(Try this: Use the phrase, "I feel..." and list as many emotions as you remember feeling during this scene.)*

If she could say what she really wants to say, what would it be?

Take a deep breath.

Remember that you are safe now. You made it. You survived.

You were strong enough and resourceful enough to do whatever you felt you had to do in order to survive.

And now, here you are. Courageously reaching back to give that little girl a chance to be heard – to cry, to scream, to feel.

Give her permission where she may not have had it before. Tell her it's ok.

She has a right to feel whatever she feels.

She has a right to want whatever she wants.

If you're feeling safe enough...take a deep breath, exhale slowly, and see if you can BE that girl in the scene.

Count backwards from 10 to 1 as you step back in time and into the experience of the little girl.

10...9...8...*(breathe and relax your head, face, neck, shoulders)*

7...6...5...*(breathe and release your arms, back, and legs)*

4...3...2...*(look out through the eyes of the little-girl you)*

1...*(breathe and let the little girl feel what she feels)*

Stay with the feelings. Don't rush up into your head; don't escape into the stories, explanations, or judgments about what you feel.

Just feel your feelings.

In the space below, capture anything else that the little-girl you might have said if she felt safe enough to speak her mind. *(Say what she's feeling. Say what she's thinking. Say what she wants.)*

How do you experience your upset feelings in your body?

Before leaving the memory, comfort the little girl as you leave her behind.

Wrap your arms around yourself, or hug your face with your hands.

Remind the little girl in you that it's all okay now.

Take a deep breath, count forward from 1 to 10 as you bring your awareness back to the present.

1...2...3...*(breathe, and remember that you're okay now)*

4...5...6...*(breathe and feel yourself returning to the present)*

7...8...9...*(feel your presence in your feet and legs, hands and arms)*

10...*(breathe presence up your spine, into your neck and head)*

Be still.

Take in the experience of the past. Acknowledge the distance that you've travelled.

Notice how your body and emotions can react to a memory almost as powerfully as to a current event.

Breathe in, and honor your courage.

Breathe out, and feel gratitude for your survival. Send a silent thank you to the universe, God, a mentor, yourself, your spirit guide whomever you credit for helping you survive.

It doesn't matter whether the event you revisited was large or small. Pain is pain. And to a little person, any pain can feel big and scary.

Unhealed childhood wounds can fester - infecting our current relationships with friends, employers, spouses, and children. They lead us to over-react to incidents that trigger old feelings.

This reflective exercise begins the self-healing process by digging up old suppressed feelings - taking them from your unconscious mind and bringing them conscious – and giving you a chance to work them OUT, instead of keeping them IN.

The first benefit of this process is **Empathy for Ourselves**. This exercise isn't about wallowing in self-pity, or blaming others. It is about honoring how far we've come. And celebrating our gratitude to the spiritual and physical forces that helped us survive.

The second benefit of the above exercise is **Empathy for Our Children**. Seeing life again through the eyes of a child, remembering our childhood feelings and thoughts, puts us in touch with how children experience life. This helps us to be more mindful of what we say and do, because we're conscious of how they might experience our actions.

Now that you've revisited the painful memory, let's acknowledge its meaning in your life so far.

Trial-to-Treasure Step 2: Acknowledge the Effect

Typically, draining the pain out of a memory allows you to look at the memory more objectively.

Before uncovering the lesson this memory can teach you today, take a moment to acknowledge how this memory has shaped you until now.

❖　❖　❖　❖　❖　❖　❖　❖　❖　❖　❖　❖　❖　❖　❖

Exercise 1.2: Acknowledge How Events Shaped You

Summarize what you learned about **yourself** AT THE TIME of
the event you just described.

What **thoughts** about yourself were planted in your head as a result of this experience?

What feelings did you begin to hold about yourself during the event?

Summarize what you learned about **others** AT THE TIME of this event.

What did you think about the specific person or people involved?

What ideas formed about what people (parents, grownups, men, women) are like?

What feelings did you begin to hold about people like that?

Summarize what you learned about the way the world works AT THE TIME of the event. What did this event teach you about "the way things are," or "the way life is?"

How did this event shape your feelings about life, or about the world?

Like the previous exercise, this one sharpens our sense of empathy for ourselves and for our children.

Negative, limiting beliefs we hold about ourselves, others, and life in general are most likely based on painful events that happened in the past. Our beliefs are not "Truth." They are explanations our child-brains created to explain why things were happening to us.

As grownups, remembering the childhood events that shaped our beliefs, we are now free to re-interpret the assumptions we made back then, and to let go of the beliefs that keep us from moving forward.

That is how this work heals both us and our families. We get to re-parent ourselves as we determine the kind of parents we want to be for our children.

We get to heal our wounds as we learn not to inflict similar wounds on our kids.

As we acknowledge the effects of others' insensitivity, we consciously decide to be more sensitive parents.

This takes us to the final step: Uncovering the Treasure.

Trial-to-Treasure Step 3: Uncover the Treasure

Comb through this memory one last time. This time, from your present-day perspective as a mother.

What does this memory teach you about who you want to be as a parent?

❖ ❖ ❖ ❖ ❖ ❖ ❖ ❖ ❖ ❖ ❖ ❖ ❖ ❖ ❖

Exercise 1.3: Uncovering the Treasure of Parenting Wisdom

Reviewing each event one last time, ask the following questions:

What did I need most when this event was happening?

What does this teach me about what kids need?

How can I be sure my kid gets what he/she needs?

Who was there for me to turn to back then? Who would listen?

How can I ensure my child feels seen and heard? What kind of relationships are important for my child to have – with me and with others?

What did I want most back then?

How can I tune in and learn what's most important to my child? How can I best provide for my child's needs for emotional safety?

What are some of the indirect ways I tried to communicate my pain back then?

How can I stay tuned into my child so I can understand his/her indirect ways of telling me something important?

How valued/cherished did I feel?

What are some ways I can ensure that my child feels valued and loved?

This final step, "Uncovering the Treasure," is, the only good reason to hold on to and reflect on the past.

The past is over. It is done.

There are things that were out of your control back then. You were small, vulnerable, and dependent on others for your safety and well-being.

You found ways to cope with the hand you were dealt.

You were a child, and nothing that happened to you was your fault.

However, who you choose to be FROM THIS DAY FORWARD, is up to you.

Your past does not dictate your future.

The only good purpose the past can serve is to guide you in creating a better present and future.

Delving into your memories and learning true empathy for children, transforms pain into promise.

You can heal yourself by gaining a deeper understanding of who you've been, and a better sense of who you wish to become.

You can heal your family by consciously deciding how you will interact with them. By being aware of the potential effects of your words and deeds. And by honoring their point of view.

Learning from the Past

It's fitting that we call painful memories and their effects on us, "Baggage."

Our Baggage can be a heavy weight that slows us down and holds us back. It can become the excuse for why we can't move forward in our lives.

Using the Trial-to-Treasure process to sift through the baggage and toss out the dead weight (blame, excuses, guilt, what we wish had been), lightens the load.

What's left is simply "What Happened" or "What Was." And by studying what was, using the Trial-to-Treasure process, we can learn lessons from the past that help us create a better future.

In the end, instead of a Baggage of Trials – to lug around, and hand down to our children – we'll have uncovered a Treasure Chest of Parenting Wisdom, filled with golden nuggets of Lessons Learned.

Our kids will inherit this treasure chest, rather than the baggage. We will create a legacy of healing in our family line, rather than continuing a legacy of pain.

For review, the 3 steps of the Trial-to-Treasure process are as follows:

Step 1: Revisit (and re-experience) the memory

Step 2: Acknowledge the effects

Step 3: Uncover the Treasure

Go through this process with other painful memories. Grab another journal, and process other memories you tote around in your "Baggage."

Use the same questions, and explore the top 5 painful childhood memories that come to mind. Learn everything you can from them. Give them your loving attention, and promote your deep healing.

Seek support of a counselor, coach, or wise friend. You don't have to do this alone.

The Trial-to-Treasure process works with happy memories, as well as painful ones.

Now that we've exhausted the painful memories, and learned many good parenting lessons from them, let's look at the happy memories. There is much to be learned there as well.

Notes

Notes

Chapter 2

Celebrating What Your Mom Did Well

Chances are, no matter what mom did wrong, she did at least some things right. She baked good cookies or made a big deal out of celebrating your birthday. She taught you skills that you still use today.

Perhaps, her own childhood was less than ideal, and she did the best she could to provide a better life than she'd had.

Hopefully there is at least one thing you can look back and say that Mom did well.

However, even if you can't think of one thing that you appreciate that your mom did with you, complete the following exercises anyway.

Think of other people who were in your life as a child. Perhaps the good memories were with your grandmother, or aunt. Maybe it was your dad, or uncle.

Who was there for you?

Let's examine the highlights of your childhood. This will round out your understanding of "what works" as a parent, and give you even more insights for bringing the light into children's lives.

Let this journey into the good memories also remind you that **you don't have to do the work of parenting all by yourself.** The more people in your child's life, confirming and reflecting his or her goodness, the better.

So, as you think about the good Mom did, and the joy others brought to your childhood experience, be mindful of how important it is for your children to have other mentors, besides you, who will support them in knowing and loving themselves.

Step 1: Revisit the Memory

When you think back to the times in your childhood when you were happiest, what memories come up first? What was happening when your smile was the biggest? Who was there? What did they do to make this event so memorable?

Whether the memory is a specific event, or an aspect of your childhood that was handled well, go into that experience and see how much it can teach you about what is important to do with your children.

Exercise 2.1: Revisit the Joyful Memory

What's the first happy scene that comes to mind when you remember your childhood fondly?

What did your mom, or another, do that you especially liked?

Go back to that time. Step into that memory. Really give yourself a chance to be back there and enjoy it as if it is happening again, right now.

Count backwards from 10 to 1, and as you do, slip further out of this time and deeper into the memory.

10...9...8...*(breathe and relax your head, face, neck, shoulders)*

7...6...5...*(breathe and release your arms, back, and legs)*

4...3...2...*(look out through the eyes of the little-girl you)*

1...*(breathe and feel everything that the little girl feels)*

BE in that scene. What is happening? What do you see?

What do you smell? Taste? Hear? What do you feel on your skin? Describe every detail you can remember.

What are you feeling in your heart?

What are you thinking in your head – is it words? Is it pictures? Write every word, draw every image that represents what you're feeling in this memory.

Capture anything else that comes to mind.

Don't filter. Don't analyze. Just record.

If it feels right, hug yourself tight and celebrate this good experience.

Loving experiences like this probably played a huge role in your survival. Give thanks for every drop of joy that washed into your life.

Take a deep breath, count forward from 1 to 10 as you bring your awareness back to the present.

1...2...3...*(breathe, and remember hold on to the joy you feel)*

4...5...6...*(breathe and bring that joy into the present)*

7...8...9...*(feel joyous presence in your feet and legs, hands and arms)*

10...*(breathe joy up your spine, into your neck and head)*

Wasn't that fun?

Do you notice the difference between how you feel after revisiting a happy memory and how you feel after revisiting a painful memory?

Remembering the good brings on such a rush of pleasure, we could probably use good memories as "drugs." When you're feeling bad, conjure up a good memory. Escape into it. Bring that joy into your spirit and share it liberally with others.

Repeat this exercise exploring at least half as many happy memories as the painful ones you examined earlier.

If possible, try to revisit even *more* happy memories than you did painful ones.

As mentioned earlier, these joyful memories could be specific events, like the time your mom stood up for you against misguided teacher. Or it could be parenting choices your mom made that you recognize had a good effect on you, like making sure you had your own room, or handling sibling disputes fairly.

Again, if mom didn't have one single redeeming quality – which would be extremely rare –think of other positive people or events that crossed your path. Was school the place you felt most rewarded? Was it a sport or a coach that brought out the best in you?

Remembering the people and events that brought us joy as children can remind us how important it is for our children to have great, loving experiences to grow on.

Step 2: Acknowledge the Effect

Now, as you did with the painful memories, go back into each scene or event listed. Explain what they did for you, how they added to you as a person. What did these memories teach you about yourself? About others? About the world?

❖ ❖ ❖ ❖ ❖ ❖ ❖ ❖ ❖ ❖ ❖ ❖ ❖ ❖ ❖

Exercise 2.2: How Joyful Experiences Shaped You

Summarize what you learned about **yourself** AT THE TIME of the event.

What thoughts about yourself were planted in your head as a result of this experience?

What feelings did you begin to hold about yourself during the event?

Summarize what you learned about **others** AT THE TIME of the event.

What did you think about the specific person or people involved?

What ideas formed about what people (parents, grownups, men, women) are like?

What feelings did you begin to hold about people like that?

For each event, summarize what you learned about the way the
world works AT THE TIME of the event.

What did this event teach you about "the way things are," or "the way life is?"

How did this event shape your feelings about life, or about the world?

The exercise above is identical to Exercise 1.2, for our positive experiences shape us as surely as our negative ones.

Sometimes we seem to notice more readily the marks left by life's beatings than the indentations left by life's hugs.

Look at who you are. Your beauty. Your strength. The things you do best. The parts of your personality that you love most.

They developed not only *in spite* of your childhood, but were inspired by some of your most favorite, cherished childhood experiences.

Step 3: Uncover the Treasure

Finally, review your positive childhood experiences with the eyes of a mother. Learn every delicious insight you'd like to bring into your relationship with your child.

❖ ❖ ❖ ❖ ❖ ❖ ❖ ❖ ❖ ❖ ❖ ❖ ❖ ❖ ❖

Exercise 2.3: Learning What To Do As A Mother

Reviewing each event one last time, ask the following questions:

What did I enjoy most about this event or the decision made by
the adults involved?

What does this teach me about the significance of joy and pleasure in my child's life?

What was so special about this event that it stayed with me this long?

How might I help my child develop good memories that last a lifetime – good memories that have a greater effect than any painful memories?

What does this memory remind me about what I find "fun?"

How do I arrange to have "fun" these days? Am I having enough fun? Could there be more? How can I fulfill my desire for fun in my life – both with and without my children?

With whom did I have the most fun as a kid? What made being
with them so much fun?

How might I bring a similar quality into my relationship with my child? How will my child remember me as "fun?"

There's no such thing as a childhood with too much laughter. While we want our kids to be competent, disciplined, and responsible – we also want them to be happy.

Be conscious of how great a role you play in bringing joy into your child's life.

Be mindful of how you can use your words and actions to help your child feel cherished and capable.

Expose your child to others who love him or her. Provide plenty of loving interactions so your child learns that he/she is infinitely lovable.

Fostering healthy, happy relationships with our children helps them to develop equally healthy, happy relationships with others.

That may be the most important life skill of all.

Honoring the Good

Spending as much (or more) time remembering the good as we do remembering the bad is the key to healing relationships.

Our relationships say a lot about us: The healthier they are, the healthier we are.

The healthier we are, the better moms we can be.

Notes

Notes

Notes

Chapter 3

Forgiving Mom, Healing Yourself

Note: We're focusing here on moms, only because of the title of the main book, *Becoming the Mom I Wish I'd Had*. However, your mom may not have been the only one (or the main one) whose mistakes brought pain into your childhood experience.

Remember, this journal is YOUR SPACE. Adjust the text to reflect your experience.

Moms are People, Too

Newsflash: Moms can be wrong. Moms are human. Moms are fallible. **Moms make mistakes.**

Their actions are based on their personal history, their cultural and religious beliefs, and sometimes the latest trends in childrearing.

Moms can be well-intentioned, yet mis-directed.

However, even though your mom may have done the best she knew how to do, it doesn't negate your experience.

Both things are true:

- Your mom had a set of circumstances, assumptions, and issues, and

- You had your own feelings, thoughts, and beliefs that developed in reaction to her behavior toward you.

These truths exist simultaneously. Your perspective doesn't make her perspective untrue. And hers doesn't make yours untrue.

Your childhood feelings and experience are not about "right" or "wrong." You don't have to prove she was wrong so that you can be right. What you felt is what you felt. Period.

No blame necessary. No judgment required.

No one can say, "You can't feel that way, because your mom was dealing with so much."

You can respect your right to your point of view, and still respect (or at least accept) that Mom had her point of view.

In fact, here's an exercise that may help you to honor your mother's circumstances.

❖ ❖ ❖ ❖ ❖ ❖ ❖ ❖ ❖ ❖ ❖ ❖ ❖ ❖ ❖

Exercise 3.1: Acknowledging Mom's Perspective

You've already described what was true for you in the previous exercises.

Now, if you like, **take a moment to describe what was true for your mom** (or whatever adult is featured in your painful memories).

From what you know, what was your mom's situation?

What was TRUE about her marital situation?

What was TRUE about her own upbringing? What was her relationship like with her mom / dad / guardians?

What did she know or believe about "children," or "childhood?"

What did she know or believe about "parenting" or "a parent's responsibility?"

As far as you know, where did her beliefs come from?

❖　❖　❖　❖　❖　❖　❖　❖　❖　❖　❖　❖　❖　❖　❖

Again, capturing what was true for your mom isn't intended to talk you out of what was true for you. It's not to encourage you to minimize your experience or dismiss it as, "not really all that bad."

The goal of this exercise is to give you permission to hold both YOUR truth and SOMEONE ELSE'S truth.

Too often we use others' perspectives to rationalize why we don't have a right to our own.

Hold both perspectives as valid and sacred.

This is the root of forgiveness.

The Healing Power of Forgiveness

We forgive others not for their sake, but for our own.

Forgiveness means letting go. Accepting the past instead of arguing with it.

What happened, happened.

Denying what happened, or your feelings about it, dishonors yourself. Denial pushes your true feelings deep under the surface. They don't disappear. They unconsciously affect your relationships with others and yourself.

On the flip side, holding on to resentment toward others is often an attempt to punish the other indefinitely. It is our attempt to ensure that whoever offended us doesn't get away with it.

But if we imprison others with our blame, we remained imprisoned also. We're like a jailer who's keeping an eye on the prisoner...but has to stay in jail, to do so.

Forgiveness frees us to take the life we've been given and make the most of it.

Forgiveness frees us to find the treasure in our past trials. To make our pain productive. To move forward rather than chain ourselves to the past.

Explore the following "Forgiveness" exercises ONLY WHEN YOU ARE READY.

Don't say what is not true for you. Don't force yourself to lie.

If there are small parts of your experience that you can forgive your mom for, then admit to only those parts.

If you are not in a genuine state of forgiveness, skip this exercise, and return to it when you are ready.

❖ ❖ ❖ ❖ ❖ ❖ ❖ ❖ ❖ ❖ ❖ ❖ ❖ ❖ ❖

Exercise 3.2: Forgiving Mom

Holding both your perspective, and your mom's perspective, look into your heart and observe what you are able to forgive about your mom.

In the space below, write, "Mom, I forgive you for..." and list the shortcomings and mistakes in judgment that you can honestly forgive.

❖ ❖ ❖ ❖ ❖ ❖ ❖ ❖ ❖ ❖ ❖ ❖ ❖ ❖ ❖

Forgiving Your Past Self

Forgiving others also helps us forgive ourselves.

Many people, who emerge from severely or mildly abusive childhoods, carry with them some level of guilt. We think, "If only I had behaved better...", "If only I had spoken up...", or "If only I weren't so passive..."

We spend our lives believing that we had more control over the situation than we did.

When you're young, small, vulnerable, and dependent, the power doesn't rest with you. **Everything you do, as a kid, is your best effort to get your needs met.**

Even if you misbehaved. Even if you did things you knew were bad. Even if you submitted to mistreatment. YOU WERE THE CHILD. The adults around you lacked the skills to do better. They may have failed you – perhaps unwittingly.

But you were an innocent child doing the best you could to find love and security.

If this next exercise doesn't apply to you, skip forward to the next one. However, if you have ever experienced any guilt about things you did or experienced as a kid, try this.

❖   ❖   ❖   ❖   ❖   ❖   ❖   ❖   ❖   ❖   ❖   ❖   ❖   ❖   ❖

Exercise 3.3: Forgiving Your Past Self

Find a photograph of yourself as a kid.

Look at that little-girl you.

What was she like?

What needs of hers were not being met?

What did she have to put up with that she didn't understand?

What did she do that SHE felt was wrong? What did she do that YOU'VE always felt was wrong?

With all the love and compassion in your heart for that little girl in the picture, and with the perspective you now have as an adult –

Write, "I forgive myself for..." and list anything you have harbored guilt about in your heart, which you can now forgive.

Forgiving Your Present Self

As sure as you're human, you will make mistakes.

Forgiving others is great practice for forgiving yourself, and vice versa.

Forgiving others, and yourself, is also a great way to model healthy relationships for our kids.

We can teach our kids to forgive by being open to feedback, and eager to apologize when we've missed the mark.

It's hard to admit we might be wrong, when we don't practice forgiveness of ourselves and others.

With forgiveness as our natural state of being, we can feel good and lovable even when we're imperfect.

More importantly, we can assure our kids that they are good and lovable, even when they're imperfect. (It's what we call "unconditional love.")

Like "Honesty," "Determination" and other great qualities we want to pass on to our kids, "Forgiveness" is a quality we must live in order to give.

If you have already been a mother long enough to make mistakes (say, longer than a day), celebrate your unconditional love for yourself through the following act of forgiveness.

❖ ❖ ❖ ❖ ❖ ❖ ❖ ❖ ❖ ❖ ❖ ❖ ❖ ❖ ❖

Exercise 3.4: Forgiving Your Present Self

Alright, 'fess up. What did you do?

For just a moment, slap on your Self-Judgment cap, and name the things you now wish you hadn't done to your kid.

Now, whip the Self-Judgment cap off. (Burn it.)

Remember all the compassion you were able to muster for the little-girl you? Spread it on over to the big-girl you.

As Maya Angelou said, "You did the best you knew how to do. And when you knew better, you did better."

Write, "I forgive myself for…" and, as honestly as you can, list every offense you listed on the previous page.

Hug and love yourself. And rejoice that you're turning over a new leaf as a parent.

❖ ❖ ❖ ❖ ❖ ❖ ❖ ❖ ❖ ❖ ❖ ❖ ❖ ❖ ❖

Whether our mothers ask forgiveness or not, whether they admit they were wrong or not, the sooner we forgive and accept our moms as human and fallible – even when we most needed them to be perfect – the sooner we can heal.

The more deeply we heal ourselves, the more emotionally healthy we can be for our children.

We can heal ourselves...heal our families...and heal the world by adding more happy, confident, emotionally healthy young people to the population.

Now, that you've learned the lessons of the past, it's time to assess the present and prepare for the future.

The remainder of this journal will guide you through the principles and tools of the HEART-Based Parenting Approach.

You'll have plenty of space to explore how the principles apply to you directly, and to design your parenting approach "With the End in Mind."

Notes

Notes

Notes

~ Part II ~

Looking Forward

Becoming the Mom You Wish You'd Had

Chapter 4

Parenting With the End in Mind

Parenting can be so stressful that we simply do what works the fastest, with no thought about the long-term consequences.

We let the baby "cry it out" for a few days, so we can have years of quiet nights – but we don't consider how abandoned the baby might feel and how the emotional distance might affect his relationship with us in the teen years.

We smack the 5-year-old in the mouth for saying something we dislike – without thinking we may be teaching her to accept physical abuse in future relationships.

Our children's psyche and self-esteem, as well as their long-term relationship with us, are shaped by these little short-term actions. The more thought we give to our ultimate goal – how we'd like our children to feel about themselves and us – the more we'll make choices that support the result we desire.

As Dr. Phil says: *You're not raising kids, you're raising adults.* The choices you make today should reflect your highest vision for your child tomorrow.

What kind of adults do you want your kids to turn out to be? Do you want them to be self-loving, or self-critical? Would you like them to confidently follow their hearts and make value-based decisions, or to follow the crowd for fear of making a mistake?

In the following exercise, you'll explore the question, "What kind of qualities would I like my children to possess 10 years from now?"

It can be easier to see 10 years into the future. If your child is a newborn, you may want to project 20 years ahead, then work back to 10.

Exercise 4.1: Your Child in 10 Years

Close your eyes, and picture the qualities you would like your child to possess 10 years from now. Then answer the following questions.

Ten years from now, when my child is ____ years old, I would like her/him to have the following general qualities:

1.

2.

3.

4.

5.

6.

7.

8.

9.

10.

The list of qualities might include *Responsible, Peaceful, Happy, Committed, Playful, Helpful, Respectful, Loving, Confident, Productive, Thrifty, Strong, Carefree, etc.*

Gandhi told us to "Be the change we want to see in the world."
You must also "Be" the change you want to see in your family.

What are some ways you can BE the example of the above
qualities?

How will you handle the routine issues of parenthood (bedtime, tantrums, potty training, sibling rivalry, mealtimes, chores, etc) in a way that **helps your child develop these qualities**?

How will you help your child recognize and strengthen these qualities in him-/herself? (What will you do or say when you catch your kid in the act of illustrating these great qualities?)

<u>Friends</u>

Who would you like your child to be (or What qualities would you like him/her to illustrate) in his/her FRIENDSHIPS?

Gandhi told us to "Be the change we want to see in the world." You must also "Be" the change you want to see in your family.

What are some ways you can BE the example of the above qualities?

How will you handle the routine issues of parenthood (sibling rivalry, sharing, communicating wants and needs, etc) in a way that **helps your child develop these qualities?**

How will you help your child recognize and strengthen these qualities in him-/herself? (What will you do or say when you catch your kid in the act of illustrating these great qualities?)

Education

Who would you like your child to be (or What qualities or beliefs would you like him/her to illustrate) when it comes to EDUCATION?

What are some ways you can BE the example of the above qualities?

How will you handle the routine issues of parenthood (reading, learning, school performance, etc.) in a way that **helps your child develop these qualities**?

How will you help your child recognize and strengthen these qualities in him-/herself? (What will you do or say when you catch your kid in the act of illustrating these great qualities?)

<u>Money</u>

Who would you like your child to be (or What qualities or beliefs would you like him/her to illustrate) when it comes to MONEY?

What are some ways you can BE the example of the above qualities?

How will you handle the routine issues of parenthood (gifts, allowance, spending, etc.) in a way that **helps your child develop these qualities**?

How will you help your child recognize and strengthen these qualities in him-/herself? (What will you do or say when you catch your kid in the act of illustrating these great qualities?)

❖ ❖ ❖ ❖ ❖ ❖ ❖ ❖ ❖ ❖ ❖ ❖ ❖ ❖ ❖

Once you have a clear picture of the end result of your parenting, that picture can guide every decision you make.

Every interaction with our children helps shape the adults they will become. We only have these little people for 18 years or so, but what we do with them can reverberate for the rest of their lives, and the lives of generations to come.

Whether we parent consciously or unconsciously, the fact remains that our actions WILL affect who they become. Our interactions with them today WILL set the tone of our relationship with them tomorrow.

Being mindful about your parenting, acting with thought and intention rather than haphazardly, increases the chances that you'll like the results, that you'll be proud of how you handled the ominous responsibility of parenting.

Picturing Your Relationship 10 Years From Now

What do you feel is the most important thing you can give your kid?

Here's a hint: It isn't the latest techno-gadgets, or even the best education money can buy.

More than anything, kids need a great relationship with their parents.

The knowledge that you love them and think the world of them will anchor your children through any of life's potential storms. Good grades or bad, lots of friends or few, your relationship can be a haven, a place where your kid always feels seen, heard, and accepted just for being himself.

Such a relationship is a good model for your child's relationships with others, and with himself.

As parents, we have a unique opportunity to teach our kids how to build healthy relationships by developing a healthy relationship with them.

Our adult children will be better equipped to lovingly talk through differences with their life partners if we teach them how to do it. They will know how to have loving relationships free of blaming, criticizing or manipulating, if our relationship with them is free of these obstacles, too.

Earlier you envisioned the qualities you want your child to possess down the road.

This time, picture the RELATIONSHIP between you and your child. What would you like it to be 10 years from now?

❖ ❖ ❖ ❖ ❖ ❖ ❖ ❖ ❖ ❖ ❖ ❖ ❖ ❖ ❖

Exercise 4.2: Your Relationship With Your Child in 10 Years

Close your eyes, and picture the relationship you would like to have with your child 10 years from now. Then answer the following questions.

Ten years from now, when my child is _____ years old, I would like our relationship to be like this:

<u>10 Years From Now</u>

It's 10 years from now. Your kid is _____ years old.

What does your child enjoy most about you?

What kinds of things do you do together?

How do you reconnect when you seem to be growing distant?

Present Day

What can you do today that will move your relationship one step closer to this 10-year vision?

❖   ❖   ❖   ❖   ❖   ❖   ❖   ❖   ❖   ❖   ❖   ❖   ❖   ❖   ❖

The relationship you want with your child in the future begins today.

If you want your child's respect, start by respecting her.

If you want your child to listen, listen to her.

If you want her to understand your love and concern for her, show her you understand her point of view.

Remember this poem, written by Diana Haskins Sterling, author of *Parent as Coach.* Although it was written based on the work she did with teenagers, it beautifully sums up what kids need from parents at any age.

A Message to Parents
If you respect me, I will hear you
If you listen to me, I will feel understood
If you understand me, I will feel appreciated
If you appreciate me, I will know your support
If you support me as I try new things, I will become responsible
And when I am responsible, I will grow to be independent
In my independence, I will grow to love you
and respect you all of my life.
Love, Your Teenager
(*Diana Haskins Sterling*)

Our ultimate goal as parents is to raise responsible, independent adults, not compliant, obedient children. We want to usher off into the world adults who feel good about themselves and who feel competent to create the lives they want.

We want school-aged kids and teenagers who do what's right even when no one is looking. We want adult children with whom we can enjoy positive lifelong relationships.

Our parenting choices today should reflect the outcomes we want tomorrow.

In the next chapter, you'll explore The 3 Fundamental Beliefs that can support you in creating a mutually loving and respectful relationship with your children.

Notes

Notes

Notes

Chapter 5

The HEART-Based Parenting Approach
~ 3 Fundamental Principles ~

HEART-Based vs POWER-Based Parenting

Which types of tools fill your parenting toolkit: POWER-Based tools, or HEART-Based Tools?

More often than not, do you (or will you) resort to POWER-Based tools, like shaming, yelling, hitting, punishing, manipulating, and criticizing to get your kid to do what you want?

POWER-Based parenting methods Promote Obedience While Encouraging Resentment. They use the force of our size and authority to compel children to obey.

Two of the biggest drawbacks to POWER-Based parenting are:

1. Alienation and Distancing – Power struggles make enemies of parents and kids. Parents develop a Win-Lose mindset, believing they must "win" in the battle of wills, and their kids, therefore, must "lose."

2. Lack of Self-Discipline – Learning to obey out of fear of punishment delays kids' ability to develop self-discipline, or an internal motivation for good behavior. When reasons for behaving are all external, what's the motivation to do right when no one's watching or when they could get away with doing wrong? They fail to learn how to tune into the inner voice

By contrast, HEART-Based Parenting means parenting with **Honesty, Empathy, Appreciation, Respect and Time**.

With HEART-Based Parenting, we are mindful that our words and actions build our children up instead of tearing them down. We parent our kids from the inside out – instilling self-discipline instead of external discipline. We *inspire* good behavior instead of *enforcing* it.

The HEART-Based Parenting approach is conscious, sensitive, and empathic. It assures kids that we're on their side, instead of assuming that we're enemies. It promotes Win-Win outcomes, rather than Win-Lose.

How strongly do the five principles and the 3 Foundational Beliefs of the HEART-Based Parenting Approach resonate with you? How do they show up in your parenting?

❖ ❖ ❖ ❖ ❖ ❖ ❖ ❖ ❖ ❖ ❖ ❖ ❖ ❖ ❖

Exercise 5.1: Parenting from the HEART

<u>Honesty</u> - *Expressing ourselves lovingly and honestly with our children, and creating an environment where they feel safe being honest with us.*

How safe does/will your child feel it is to be honest with you? What is (or will be) your evidence of that?

How might saying things like, "I feel afraid watching you do that," as opposed to, "Stop jumping down those stairs right now," affect the level of honesty in your relationship with your child?

<u>Empathy</u> – *Being able to understand and honor our children's feelings and points of view. Modeling for them how to do the same with us and with others.*

How would you like to see your child express empathy for him-/herself and others?

How could you show your child that you understand and
honor his/her feelings and perspective – even if it differs from
yours?

<u>Appreciation</u> – *Letting our children know how happy we are to have them in our lives and how their special gifts enrich the family.*

How would you like to see your child express appreciation and gratitude in her/his everyday life?

What kinds of things can you do to make it abundantly clear
to your child that she/he is appreciated as a person, and for
the contributions she/he makes?

<u>Respect</u> – *Treating our children as people, not possessions. Celebrating and promoting their individuality. Giving the respect we wish to receive.*

How would you like to receive your child's respect? What would it look like?

What are some ways you can show respect for your child as an individual, as a fellow human being?

<u>Time</u> – *Showing our kids how important they are to us by spending time having fun with them, and getting to know them. Also, being patient with them as they make mistakes and learn the game of life.*

Forty years from now, how would you like your kid to look back on the time you two spent together? What memories would you like him/her to hold dear?

How can you use time (quality and quantity) to express love for your children?

❖ ❖ ❖ ❖ ❖ ❖ ❖ ❖ ❖ ❖ ❖ ❖ ❖ ❖ ❖

Beliefs → Interpretation → Response

What you believe about people shows up in your behavior towards them. If you believe someone is untrustworthy, she'll feel distrust in your treatment of her. If you believe someone is interesting, he'll sense it in your approach.

Our beliefs guide our actions. They also guide how we interpret another's behavior, and how we respond.

When adults hold the following beliefs about children, they feel unconditionally loved, deeply understood, and fully respected:

1. The Belief in Children's Goodness
2. The Belief in Children as Unfolding Mysteries
3. The Belief in Children's Need to Learn from Experience

What are your beliefs about children in general? Examine them here. Then address your beliefs about your child specifically in the following chapters.

Exercise 5.2: Fundamental Beliefs about Children

<u>Children and Goodness</u>

Based on your life experience, what are the beliefs you hold about children? Answer by completing the following sentences with as many descriptors as come to mind. (Be honest, include both your positive, and negative beliefs.)

Children are...

Children need...

Circle the most positive beliefs about the nature and needs of children that you listed above.

If adults only held these positive beliefs about children – if we only saw children as good – how would we respond to them, even if they're "mis-behaving?"

How might this approach bring out the good in children?

Children as Unfolding Mysteries

What's your belief about the role of an adult in a kid's life? What do kids need from us? How can we best support them in becoming who they are meant to be?

How does approaching a kid as "a mystery" differ from approaching a kid with a fixed idea about what he/she must become?

Who might you have become if the adults in your life encouraged you to explore and define your unique path?

Children Learning from Experience

How do you interpret children's "misbehavior?" What do kids do that's "wrong" and why do they do it, in your opinion?

How might accepting kids' misbehavior as "mistakes" instead of "offenses" affect adults' behavior toward them?

How might this approach affect kids' view of themselves? of their purpose and place in the world? of adults?

These 3 Fundamental Beliefs – the belief in children's **goodness**, the belief in children as **unfolding mysteries,** and the belief in children's need to **learn from experience** – lay a firm foundation on which to develop a healthy relationship with children.

These **3 Fundamental Beliefs** lead adults to interpret children's behavior in the most positive light. Helping us to respond from the HEART, rather than from a place of POWER.

Our loving responses foster a relationship that feels safe for our children to learn to know, love, and express their uniqueness in the world.

How can you reflect these fundamental beliefs in your everyday interactions with your child?

How can your words and actions help your kid to feel unconditionally loved, deeply understood, and fully respected?

In the remaining chapters, you'll apply the 9 Parenting Tools of the HEART-Based approach to your child.

Notes

Notes

Chapter 6

The 3 Parenting Tools that Illustrate the Belief in Your Child's Goodness

Have you ever seen a baby with low self-esteem? Have you ever seen one who thinks he doesn't deserve to get what he wants?

Ever seen a newborn girl hide her chubby thighs, or a 3-month-old doubt he was smart enough to roll over?

No. Babies are not born with a low self-image. They don't judge themselves as good or bad. They simply *are*. They exist. And that's enough.

They don't question their worth, intelligence, or goodness. They are fully themselves, unapologetically.

How do kids develop self-esteem issues, then? When do they begin to feel bad about what they do, what they want, and who they are? How do they come to doubt their ability to learn or to be loved?

We teach them.

By ignoring a baby's need to be held, or a toddler's need for self-expression, we teach them to believe they are defective. That they don't deserve to have what they need or want.

When we are unloving, children conclude that they are unlovable. When we treat them badly, they believe they are bad.

On the other hand, when we respect their needs, and behave lovingly toward them, they feel loved. They believe they are lovable. We treat them well and they believe they are good.

Children don't judge themselves as good or bad until we project those judgments onto them, through our loving or hostile interactions with him.

Firmly believing in our children's goodness helps us to uncover the need behind their behavior, and to acknowledge and respect those needs.

This belief is illustrated with the following 3 Parenting Tools: **Empathy, Responsiveness,** and **Closeness.** Let's look at each of these separately.

HEART-Based Parenting Approach Toolkit – Tool 1: Empathy

The cornerstone of any good relationship is Empathy.

Empathy is the ability to honor another's feelings without judgment. To respect their pain, or their joy. To understand their point of view, even if it differs from yours.

When we firmly believe our children are good, we are less likely to interpret their mistakes as malicious.

If the kid does something we disagree with, we look underneath the behavior to see what's motivating it. We help them find a healthier way of meeting that need.

Parents who believe that children are bad and must be taught to be good, tend to have a minimal sense of empathy. They can't see life from the child's perspective. They can't respond from a place of sensitivity.

Instead, they stick with their own perspective, focus on how the kids' behavior embarrasses or inconveniences them as adults, and react from a place of self-interest.

Parents who have little or no empathy see only the "wrong" in their children's inconvenient behaviors. Everything from crying babies to fighting siblings is seen an evil to be trained or beaten out of them.

This leaves the child's needs unacknowledged and unmet.

Some kids resort to behavior that is more offensive in a more desperate attempt to be heard. Other kids drive their feelings underground and resign themselves to being misunderstood.

On the other hand, when we firmly believe that children are fundamentally good – that they are good little people with good hearts and good intentions – we can accept their feelings without judging them. We can respond to their needs without questioning their motives.

When we accept kids' feelings and their point of view, we can act out of love, and not out of fear of being manipulated, or fear of losing the "battle of wills."

Empathy helps us feel and act tenderly toward our children, even when we feel annoyed by their behavior.

Parenting with empathy, we support our children's right to feel what they feel and think what they think – even if it's inconvenient for us.

This doesn't mean that we give in to every whim. Nor that we satisfy every need immediately...just that we acknowledge the need, continue to see the child as good, and approach him/her with gentleness and sensitivity.

Empathy is the most important tool in the HEART-Based Parenting toolkit. Everything else stems from it.

How can you ensure that you approach your child from a place of empathy?

Complete the exercises that relate to your child's current/future age. You may also reminisce about a previous stage.

Exercise 6.1: Tapping the Power of Empathy

<u>Newborns</u>

Imagine you were abruptly transported to an alien planet, run by giants who speak a language you don't understand.

Your arms and legs don't work in this atmosphere. You are completely dependent on these giants to meet everyone of your needs including the need to feel safe and to relieve any discomfort. And you haven't a clue how to get them to understand you.

Describe the kinds of feelings you might have.

What could the giants do to help you feel less scared and frustrated, and more comfortable and safe?

What does this say about what your newborn needs, even during crying spells, or at nighttime?

<u>Toddlers</u>
What do you imagine the world looks like from your toddler's point of view?

If she/he had enough language skills, what would your toddler say she/he wants and needs? (Remember, this is **the toddler's perspective**, not yours.)

When you need to set boundaries or say "No," how can you do it in a way that lets your toddler know you truly understand her/his feelings and desires?

How might *Empathy* with your toddler lay the groundwork for a better-than-average relationship with this kid during the teen years?

School-Aged / Teens

What do you imagine **your home environment** looks and feels like from your school-aged/teen-aged child's point of view? (Include positive and negative views.) ~ *[Alternate exercise: ASK your child.]*

What do you imagine **school** looks and feels like from your school-aged/teen-aged child's point of view? (Include positive and negative views.) ~ *[Alternate exercise: ASK your child.]*

Next time your child is describing any situation, ask questions like, "What was that like for you? What did you want most in that situation? What did you learn about yourself?"

Resist the urge to give advice, opinions, or praise.

What do you observe about your child or the interaction?

What do you observe about yourself when you do this?

Ask your child, "On a scale of 1 to 10, how well do you feel I 'get' your point of view?" Then ask, "What would push that up to a 10 (or 11)?"

What are some ways you can show this child that you understand his/her perspective, even when setting boundaries, or saying, "No?"

❖ ❖ ❖ ❖ ❖ ❖ ❖ ❖ ❖ ❖ ❖ ❖ ❖ ❖ ❖

HEART-Based Parenting Approach Toolkit –
Tool 2: Responsiveness

The most natural result of empathy is Responsiveness.

When you can feel the need behind your child's behavior, then you can respond to the need and not react to the behavior.

Responding lovingly to our children's needs affirms that they are good and their needs are important to us. They learn that, even when their tactics are annoying, we know that at their core, they are good.

When we react to a kid's surface behavior, we miss the opportunity to address the need below the surface. We miss a chance to bond with them and show the strength of our love.

We risk alienating them, leaving their needs unmet, and having them resort to less healthy behaviors in her attempt to be heard.

Remember, responding to needs doesn't mean satisfying every want.

A child who *wants* candy for breakfast, still *needs* good nutrition instead. As parents, we can empathize with the child's desire for candy – what adult hasn't eaten a donut for breakfast, at least once? But we can respond to the *need* for nourishment by supplying real food.

(A highly aware parent might even overhear that an intense craving for sweets can indicate a vitamin deficiency, and therefore, add more veggies and fruit to the kid's diet – again, responding to the *need* behind the behavior.)

Parenting responsively calls us to be insightful and inquisitive. It keeps us open to information coming from our children, our instincts, and the environment.

Most of all, parenting responsively is an expression of the belief in our child's goodness.

Responsiveness communicates unconditional love. It strengthens our children's trust that we understand and accept them for who they really are, even when they can't express themselves the way they want.

How can you be more responsive to the needs behind your child's behavior?

Exercise 6.2: Practicing Responsiveness vs Reactivity

<u>Newborns</u>

When the baby is crying, how can (or how do) you tune in to get a sense of what the baby feels or needs?

When both you and the baby are tired and cranky, what are some ways that both of your needs can be met simultaneously?

Toddlers / School-Aged / Teens

What does your child do that tends to trigger a negative reaction in you?

What's the self-talk you hear in your head when you witness this behavior in your child?

If you took your child's point of view, really got into her/his head and looked out through her/his eyes, how might you interpret that behavior differently?

What are some ways you can address the "good" need behind your child's seemingly "bad" behavior?

If your child is old enough, say to her/him, "Let's brainstorm. What are some other ways for you to express how you're feeling or say what you need?"

Let your child come up with the first (and the most) ideas. Then both of you honestly share how each idea would lead you to feel and react.

Choose options that suit both of you.

What do you observe in your child during this process?

What do you observe in yourself during this process?

❖ ❖ ❖ ❖ ❖ ❖ ❖ ❖ ❖ ❖ ❖ ❖ ❖ ❖ ❖

HEART-Based Parenting Approach Toolkit –
Tool 3: Closeness

Many parents worry that keeping their children close (physically and emotionally) will make them needy and clingy.

They fear that kids will never become self-confident individuals if kept close, so they prematurely attempt to wean kids of their dependency.

They rush to instill "*self*-sufficiency." They let babies "cry it out" so they'll learn to *self*-soothe. They ignore toddlers' cries for help, so they'll become *self*-reliant.

Then, when the kid is older and emotionally distant, parents ask, "Why won't you talk to me?" Or when the kid gets into trouble trying to manage a big problem on his own, parents ask, "Why didn't you come to me?"

In an earlier chapter, we described the relationships we'd like to have with our kids when they're older.

If we want a close relationship with them then, why not foster that closeness now?

What sense does it make to push kids away when they're little and then try to draw them in when they're older?

Even as teenagers, our kids still need to feel close to us. Many of the problems we experience with teens come from our insistence on pushing them too far away from us too soon.

When teens feel close to their parents – when they feel seen, heard, understood, and appreciated – there is less of a need to rebel.

How can you develop and maintain a close, loving relationship with your kids at any age?

Exercise 6.3: Maintaining Closeness with Kids

<u>All Ages</u>

Picture your child feeling emotionally "close" to you.

What does it look like?

What would be the advantages of having a "close" relationship with your child? (Include advantages for both you and your child.)

What disadvantages might come from this level of closeness?

How could they be resolved, while still maintaining closeness?

What are some things you can do now to develop closeness with your child that lasts his/her whole life?

Empathy + Responsiveness + Closeness

Kids pop out of the womb whole, perfect, and beautiful. They love themselves completely. They have no shame and reject no part of themselves.

They don't judge themselves as good or bad. They just "are."

They don't judge their needs as right or wrong. They simply do whatever it takes to get their needs fulfilled.

If their needs are fulfilled, they develop a positive self-image. They see themselves as worthy and lovable.

If their needs are not fulfilled, they tend to develop a lower self-image. They feel unworthy, and unlovable.

Seeing children as fundamentally good means interacting with them expressing Empathy + Responsiveness + Closeness.

These qualities help us stay open to our children as they develop into the unique individuals they came here to be.

When we empathize with and respond to their needs, and stay physically and emotionally close to them, our children trust that we know and love them, and they develop the confidence that they can get what they need in life.

HEART-Based Parenting is like providing a Magic Mirror for your child.

If you're old enough, you may remember the TV show Romper Room. The host would look into her Magic Mirror and "see" the kids in the viewing audience. "I see Mary, and Sally, and Johnny and Steve..."

Kids watching (with those names) felt SEEN. (Tough luck for kids with non-traditional names, though.)

Similarly, our children want to be SEEN by us. They feel most secure when they know we really see *them* – not just their flaws, not just our ideas of what they should or could be, but who they really *are*.

The 3 Parenting Tools described in the next chapter are based on the second fundamental belief of the HEART-Based Parenting Approach: The belief that each child is an **Unfolding Mystery**.

Believing in the inherent goodness of children, and honoring the mystery of who they are becoming, make us an affirming presence in our children's lives – helping them become their best selves.

Notes

Notes

Chapter 7

The 3 Parenting Tools that Illustrate the Belief in Your Child as an Unfolding Mystery

Imagine someone placed a seed in your hand and left you responsible for bringing it to its fullest potential. There's no picture or note indicating what kind of tree or plant it is to become. You are simply required to care for it as best you can and discover, as the seed slowly reveals, what it is meant to be.

A child is like that seed.

Each child comes here with his/her own unique path. Our job, as parents, is not to define the path, but to help discover it.

When kids are free to express themselves, they easily tell us everything we need to know about who they are and who they're meant to be.

When we set aside our own agendas and pay attention to our children's clues, we support them in living authentic, passionate lives. We spotlight and affirm their existing strengths instead of trying to replace them with different ones.

Parents who ignore their children's uniqueness and, instead, try to shape them to fit a certain mold, risk cutting children off from themselves, and from the parents.

They risk developing a relationship where kids don't feel seen, heard, or respected for who they are. Or worse, a relationship where the kids completely lose touch with who they are and disconnect from their own creativity.

Our responsibility as parents is to help our children grow to be what they came here to be - to provide the *space* for them to explore their uniqueness and the *tools* to develop their natural gifts.

Fostering our children's "unfolding" involves staying open to their signs, strengths, and style.

It means letting go of the notion that we know all there is to know about them.

It means letting go of the desire to chisel them into our image, or any other image, and instead, inviting them to know, love, and express themselves authentically.

Encouraging our children's mysteries to unfold means valuing **Self-Knowledge, Self-Expression,** and **Loving Communication.**

These are numbers 4, 5, and 6 of the 9 Parenting Tools of the HEART-Based Parenting Approach. Let's explore each.

HEART-Based Parenting Approach Toolkit – Tool 4: Self-Knowledge

From an early age, we applaud kids for learning everything there is to know *outside* of themselves. We're delighted when they count to 10, recite the alphabet, name the planets.

So much of kids' energy is spent learning "facts" that, many young people enter adulthood knowing a lot about many things in the world, but nearly nothing about themselves.

To paraphrase a common Bible scripture, *What does it profit a kid to gain the whole world and lose his own soul?*

Each child comes to this world with a unique path. Their preferences, strengths, and values are the clues they must follow to discover that path.

To live an authentic life – a life that fits them just right – it is just as important for kids to learn about themselves as it is for them to learn about the world around them.

Self-aware children are better equipped to make choices that reflect who they really are and who they most want to be.

Understanding who they are and what they value helpseven the youngest children make the self-directed choice to do what's right even when no adult is around.

The sooner we can promote self-discipline in our children, by helping them to connect with their inner reasons for good behavior, the less we'll need to rely on external motivators.

We can help our kids tune into themselves by making self-knowledge a priority. Like a mirror, we can help our kids reflect on their lives. Help them to see and to know themselves intimately.

Making self-knowledge a priority means it is just as important that our kids know what *they* want as it is that they know what *we* want.

It means that getting them to think about the natural consequences of their actions is equally or more important than us inventing consequences for their actions.

How can you promote deeper self-knowledge and self-awareness in your child?

❖   ❖   ❖   ❖   ❖   ❖   ❖   ❖   ❖   ❖   ❖   ❖   ❖   ❖   ❖

Exercise 7.1: Promoting Your Child's Knowledge of Self

<u>All Ages</u>

What would you like your child to know about her-/himself?

What are some things you can do and say to **support** your child in learning these things about her-/himself?

What are some things you could do or say that would **get in the way** of your child learning these things about her-/himself?

HEART-Based Parenting Approach Toolkit – Tool 5: Self-Expression

Were you allowed to express your full range of emotions as a kid? Were you as encouraged to say, "I'm angry," or "I don't like this," as you were to say, "I'm so excited," or "I love you?"

Was there space in your family to voice your feelings, thoughts, opinions, even if they differed from others?

Whether it's emotions, or hair style, or creative talent, kids must be allowed to express themselves if they are ever to discover who they are.

Self-expression is the active part of self-knowledge. When fostering self-knowledge, we encourage kids to look within, and find the truth of themselves.

To foster self-expression, we must create a safe space for children to bring the true "self" out into the world.

The family that accepts the whole person – that doesn't applaud the expression of certain parts of the self, while "booing" the expression of other parts – is a family that feels loving and safe for each family member to "unfold" into the fullness of him- or herself.

❖ ❖ ❖ ❖ ❖ ❖ ❖ ❖ ❖ ❖ ❖ ❖ ❖ ❖ ❖

Exercise 7.2: Encouraging Self-Expression

<u>All Ages</u>

What are some feelings that your child often expresses?

Circle the feelings (above) that are hardest for you to hear.

What's your knee-jerk reaction to hearing your child express the circled feelings? (I.e., What's your immediate thought or feeling, whether you express it or not?)

How can you attend to your own feelings AND support your child's healthy expression of ALL his/her feelings?

What are the behaviors, even the irksome ones, that your kid seems most attached to (e.g., drumming, humming, taking physical risks, socializing, making messes with toys or laundry, etc.)?

What might these behaviors tell you about who your child is, and what's important to him/her?

How can you create space for your child to safely, joyously express this part of who he/she is?

How can you show your kid, at any age, that you want to know what they think and feel, and that you care about what's important to them?

HEART-Based Parenting Approach Toolkit – Tool 6: Loving Communication

Parents' words can comfort or sting greater than anyone else's.

Our words tell our kids how we see them, and shape how they see themselves. If, in our words, they hear that they are lovable and fantastic, they will learn to see themselves as lovable and fantastic.

If, on the other hand, they hear us judging and criticizing, then they'll learn to judge and criticize themselves.

The truth is, our children *are* lovable and fantastic, each in his own way. Their mission is to discover their "own way" of being all the wondrous things they are.

Our words can be either stepping-stones or obstacles on our kids' road to discovering their own magic.

To help our children stay connected to the wonder of themselves, to help them to discover their mysterious potential and unfold into the best of themselves, we must be mindful of the messages we send.

How can you ensure that your words always communicate love and acceptance?

❖ ❖ ❖ ❖ ❖ ❖ ❖ ❖ ❖ ❖ ❖ ❖ ❖ ❖ ❖

Exercise 7.3: Communicating HEART-to-HEART

Apply the HEART principles – Honesty, Empathy, Appreciation, Respect, and Time, to your communication with your child.

Honesty

What are some ways you can make it safe for your child to be completely honest with you?

What things might you do or say that could prevent your child from being honest with you?

How can you express your honest feelings in a way that still supports your kids in holding and expressing their own point of view?

<u>Empathy</u>

What are some phrases you typically use (or would like to use) to let your child know you empathize with his/her feelings?

<u>Appreciation</u>

What do you appreciate most about what your child has brought into your life?

What are some ways you can communicate that appreciation to your child?

<u>Respect</u>

List the qualities or personality traits that you genuinely respect in your child.

Choose one quality or trait to highlight each week, or each month.

When your child does something that illustrates that quality, say to him/her, "I really respect your _____." Fill in the blank with the appropriate trait (e.g., enthusiasm, loyalty, tenderness, sensitivity, thoroughness, hard work, peacefulness, sincerity).

What do you observe in your child when you do this?

What do you observe in yourself when you do this?

Time

How does the amount of time you spend doing something signify how important it is to you?

What does the amount of time you spend with your child tell her/him about how important she/he is to you? (See it through the child's eyes, not your own.)

Another way to communicate love through Time is with our patience.

How can you show more patience with your child as he/she grows and learns from mistakes?

❖ ❖ ❖ ❖ ❖ ❖ ❖ ❖ ❖ ❖ ❖ ❖ ❖ ❖ ❖

When we are mindful to communicate lovingly with our children, we remain open to them as they change and grow. We support them as they figure out who they are and who they want to be.

Loving Communication means communicating with empathy. Understanding the long-range power of our words and actions. Being mindful to build them up instead of tearing them down – promoting the best in them instead of trying to stamp out the worst in them.

Judgment, labels, and harshness close us off from our kids. Kids don't feel safe "unfolding" – discovering and defining themselves – in relationships that are hurtful.

By communicating our love tenderly, we make the relationship safe for our kids to "unfold" *within* it, instead having to define themselves *outside* of it.

Self-Knowledge + Self-Expression + Loving Communication

Helping our kids connect to their unlimited potential is perhaps our most important task as parents.

Supporting our kids in **knowing** who they are and **expressing** their uniqueness in the world, as well as **lovingly communicating** our support of their individuality, helps our children to become the best young people they can be.

Coming up next, in the last chapter, we'll explore The 3 Parenting Tools that illustrate the Belief in Your Child's Need to Learn from Experience.

Notes

Notes

Chapter 8

The 3 Parenting Tools that Illustrate the Belief in Your Child's Need to Learn from Experience

To really learn about life, kids have to get involved, try new things, get bumped around a little. They sometimes have to do things wrong in order to figure out how to do things right.

If we come down hard on kids for doing wrong, or "misbehaving," we send the message that mistakes are unacceptable. We shut down the learning process.

Anyone who's new at anything is bound to make mistakes.

We welcome our kids to the game of life and mentor them into adulthood, by respecting their need to play the game and accepting the fact that they will make mistakes.

By encouraging them to explore new things and helping them learn from mistakes instead of punishing them, we keep kids engaged in the game of life. We allow them the hands-on experience they need to develop into the adults they want to be.

The remaining Parenting Tools - 7 - Exploration and Discovery; 8 – Choices; and 9 – Guidance – support our children's need to learn from hands-on experience.

HEART-Based Parenting Approach Toolkit – Tool 7: Exploration and Discovery

Exploration

Children are innately curious. They want to know everything about everything. The curiosity that drives them to explore and experiment is healthy. It promotes learning and growth.

Some parents inadvertently squash kids' natural curiosity by not allowing them to explore. Keeping babies safely locked in playpens, or preteens safely locked in the house, limits their freedom to explore and learn about the world around them.

Our fears about danger don't negate a child's need to explore and experiment. There are important things kids can't learn by just watching TV and reading books.

Instead of restricting kids' freedom of movement, it is better to mitigate the dangers as much as possible and teach them how to avoid danger and what to do if something goes wrong.

With toddlers, instead of creating a world of "no" – don't touch this, don't climb on that – we can eliminate as many hazards as possible, so they can safely satisfy their natural curiosity.

Each time their curiosity is rewarded by her learning something new – even if that new lesson involves falling from a non-threatening height – they will grow in confidence and in their ability to tackle life's challenges and discover their power over the world around them.

Discovery

There is a huge difference between *learning* and *being taught*.

"Learning" is active – we're in the driver's seat, we have theories to test and questions to answer. And when we figure out the answer, we really know it. We *own* what we know.

"Being taught" is passive – someone tells us what they think we should know and expects us to remember the info and use it where appropriate. It's not our discovery. We may not remember or understand it. We don't own it.

True knowledge comes through *active* learning. The deepest understanding comes from developing and pursuing answers to our own questions.

We love our kids so much that we want to teach them everything we think they need to know.

However, kids learn best when they *discover* the information rather than *receive* it.

You can tell a kid all day long that 2+2=4. He can repeat it, and try to remember it when asked. But when he *figures it out on his own*, when he tests it out with blocks and cars and apples and "discovers" that 2+2 always equals 4, he runs to tell you as if you didn't know. He really gets it. He owns it.

Instead of telling our kids everything, it's better to leave room for them to discover as many of life's truths as they can on their own.

How can you promote exploration and discovery in your home? How will you support your children's need to learn through hands-on experience?

Exercise 8.1: Promoting Exploration and Discovery

<u>Newborn / Toddlers</u>

Babies are scientists. Their rapidly growing brains crave new data to help them learn about the world.

The more they explore, the faster they learn.

How can you support your baby in safely exploring as much of the world as she/he can?

What could anyone do or say that would turn off the light of curiosity in your baby?

What will you say to yourself or others to encourage them NOT to do or say these things?   How will you keep your baby's environment safe for learning?

School-Aged

In school, much of kids' learning becomes passive. They're told what to learn and how to learn it.

The best learning is *active*. Discovering that 2+2=4 is much more rewarding than Remembering that 2+2=4.

If your child will spend many hours of the day passively learning, how can you provide active learning opportunities during his/her non-school hours?

Teens

The teen years are the only time when the brain is growing as fast as it did during the toddler years.

It's no wonder that teens' desire for new experiences and learning can be as insatiable as a toddler's.

What resources exist locally that can provide your teen with healthy new experiences? What organizations might engage your teen in learning and developing skills to prepare for adulthood?

The teen years are the final bridge between childhood and adulthood.   This is the time when they can learn to be responsible, and independent.

You cannot FORCE teens to become responsible and independent, but you can PROMOTE it.

What are some non-confrontational ways you can provide opportunities and expectations to promote your teen's growing independence?

HEART-Based Parenting Approach Toolkit –
Tool 8: Choices

We all want our young people to make good choices when it counts.

Our teenagers may be asked if they want a cigarette. Our 9 year olds may be tempted to join the schoolyard mob picking on the new kid. Our 5 year olds may want to chase a ball across the street.

We hope and pray that, when the time comes, and we're not around, our kids will choose to do the right thing.

Life is all about choices.

Learning to make good choices takes practice.

Before they face the big decisions that affect their health, safety, and future, we can give them loads of practice making easier choices. We can start offering choices even before they can talk.

It can seem more efficient to tell kids what to do, than to offer choices. It saves time...no drawn out discussions or tedious consequences.

However, barking out fewer commands, and instead, giving kids more opportunities to make choices helps them build "decision-making muscles" – just as letting them walk instead of carrying them all the time builds leg muscles.

The more kids practice making decisions that feel right, the more confident they (and we) become in their decision-making skills.

To be sure, there is a time for telling and a time for asking. However, we can give our kids more practice making decisions if we learn to "ask" more than we "tell."

How can you learn to "ask" more and "tell" less?

Exercise 8.2:   Providing More Choices

<u>All Ages</u>

What kinds of things are you telling (or ordering) your kid to do each day?

Circle 3 of the least important "Tells" (above). Seriously, which are the ones where you could give your kid wiggle room, without the sky falling down?

In the space below, **write at least 3 ways** that you could turn each of those into an "Ask." (Consider how you might provide two real, consequence-free options; an acceptable timeframe; or permission to say, "No.")

Remember: A command masked as a question is a lie. If there is no freedom of choice, don't Ask, Tell.

HEART-Based Parenting Approach Toolkit – Tool 9: Guidance

Punishment is a POWER tool (it Promotes Obedience While Encouraging Resentment).   It contradicts each of the 3 Fundamental Beliefs we've discussed.

In contrast to **the belief that kids are good,** punishment adheres, instead, to the belief that they are bad and must be forced to be good.

Instead of **acknowledging the child as an "unfolding mystery,"** punishment is used to enforce parents' ideas of how quickly children should become what the parents wish them to be.

And, above all, punishment thwarts kids' **need to learn about life through firsthand experience,** by penalizing the mistakes they make as they try to discover for themselves who they are and how to play the game of life.

Guidance, on the other hand, supports all 3 Fundamental Beliefs of the HEART-Based Parenting approach. It shows our kids that we believe they are good, that we trust that they (and we) will ultimately figure out who they are, and that we know they must experience making great and not-so-great decisions in order to grow.

When we guide our kids toward better choices, rather than punishing them for less acceptable ones, we spend more time building them up than tearing them down.

Teaching kids to do right just to avoid punishment trains them to be motivated from the outside in rather than the inside out.

While using guidance instead of punishment gives kids the space to learn to do what's right for its own sake.

Using Guidance to redirect kids to the "right track," means viewing their less productive choices as learning opportunities, rather than crimes.

How can you use Guidance instead of Punishment to help your kids make healthier choices?

❖ ❖ ❖ ❖ ❖ ❖ ❖ ❖ ❖ ❖ ❖ ❖ ❖ ❖ ❖

Exercise 8.3: Using Guidance Instead of Punishment

<u>All Ages</u>

Yelling, hitting, criticizing, blaming, and nagging, are some subtle and not-so-subtle ways adults punish kids for doing things we don't like.

What are some things your kid does that tend to bring a negative reaction out of you?

What's your usual reaction?

Knowing what you know about how parents' reactions can tear kids down or build them up, what are some other ways you might consider dealing with irksome behavior?

Kids' choices have natural consequences. You choose to practice skateboard stunts, the natural consequence may be a few scrapes and bruises.

The "consequences" we impose (for choices we don't like), are usually punishments in disguise. Punishments teach our kids that it's not safe to make choices.

How can you deal with inappropriate choices in a way that fosters better choices without punishment?

The HEART-Based Parenting Approach involves using the 5 principles of Honesty, Empathy, Appreciation, Respect, and Time, to develop a close, loving, intentional relationship with children.

Holding fast to the 3 Fundamental Beliefs – the Belief in Children's Goodness, the Belief that they are Unfolding Mysteries, and the Belief in their Need to Learn from Experience – we are able to replace our POWER-Based parenting tools with the 9 Tools of the HEART-Based Parenting Toolkit:

1. Empathy
2. Responsiveness
3. Closeness
4. Self-Knowledge
5. Self-Expression
6. Loving Communication
7. Discovery/Exploration
8. Choices
9. Guidance

We can heal our own childhood wounds, and, indeed, our entire family line, through the choices we make as parents.

Notes

~ CONCLUSION ~

Like the elderly mother who can miraculously lift a fallen car off her son, all mothers have the power to overcome the weight of a painful history to give our children a chance at a better life.

That's the magical power of love.

Maternal love calls us forth to be the best we can be. It inspires us to draw loving water from what may seem to be an empty well.

The more unconditional love we give to our children, the more we find we can give to ourselves.

That's the healing power of mindful, conscious, empathic, HEART-Based parenting.

Keep these 9 Tools at the top of your parenting toolkit: Empathy, Responsiveness, Closeness, Self-Knowledge, Self-Expression, Loving Communication, Discovery/Exploration, Choices, and Guidance.

Reach for them, and know that you are parenting with HEART: Honesty, Empathy, Appreciation, Respect, and Time.

Let the POWER tools rust away from disuse (those that Promote Obedience While Encouraging Resentment).

Don't lug around useless childhood memories. Either cut them loose, or put them to work.

Let the happy ones remind you of the importance of joy in a child's life – and be a source of that joy for your children.

Let the sad ones remind you of what's hurtful to a child – and take care that your words and actions nurture your children, instead of wounding them.

Forgive your mother for her shortcomings as you wish to be forgiven for yours.

Remember, to honor the good that she did, and to learn from the bad.

Become the Mom You Wish You'd Had. Heal yourself and your children. And write a new chapter in your family history.

~ ABOUT THE EDITOR ~

Venus Taylor is founder of The Family Healing Institute. She is a Certified Family Coach, who studied with some of the most highly regarded family and relationship coaches in the US, including Diana Sterling, of the Academy for Family Coach Training in Albuquerque, NM (www.familycoachtraining.com), and Dr. Susan Campbell, author of *Getting Real,* in Sebastopol, CA (www.susancampbell.com).

She earned her Master of Education from Harvard University with an emphasis on Risk and Prevention.

Venus lives with her husband, Hycel Taylor III, and two children in Boston, MA.

To learn more about her Family Healing programs, visit www.HealMyFamily.com, or email venus@HealMyfamily.com.

Printed in the United States
220331BV00001B/2/P

9 780982 318645